I0020415

Copyright Material

Table of Contents

Chapter Four: Email on Galaxy S6

Chapter Five: Contacts

Chapter Six: Browser and facebook download

Chapter Seven: Entertainment

Chapter Eight: Music and Video

Chapter Nine: Voice Assistant

Chapter Ten: Using Calendar

Chapter One: Call Function

Introduction:

In the premium build quality and design of the Galaxy S6, instead of going with a boring evolutionary design update like in years past. Samsung decided to start from Ground Zero and build something completely new, dishing the cheaper filling plastic materials that we've kind of come to associate with Samsung in favor of much more premium feeling glass and metal with jewel tone colors including white, pearl, black, sapphire and gold platinum. Both the front and the non-removable back of the galaxy s6 are covered with Gorilla Glass 4. There's a metal band that wraps all the way around the sides machine drilled holes for these speakers go at the bottom along with those stylish chamfered edges resulting in a foam that feels very high-end and it's just downright sexy to display. Welcome to Galaxy S6 techology!

Top 9 Galaxy S6 New Features!

Top 9 best new features that make both the Galaxy s6 probably the most exciting phones from Samsung since the Galaxy s3.

Screen:

Samsung finally broke its habit of making the Galaxy S 2 screen bigger year after year with the Galaxy s6 retaining the same 5.1 inch screen size that we saw in the S5 because of this Samsung was able to reduce the overall footprint of the phone by making the bezels a little bit thinner which should translate into easier one-handed use now while the screen size technically remains the same. The display itself is actually all new.

Resolution:

 Samsung bumped the resolution of its Super AMOLED display up to 2560 by 1440 or quad HD giving you a crazy PPI of 576 this is 30% higher than wolves on the S5 and a whopping 76% higher than on the iPhone 6 on top of that, the display is now over 30% brighter meaning you'll get better outdoor visibility to go along with those super sharp and super crisp visuals that you'll get from the screen.

Performance:

So Samsung phones with their heavy TouchWiz have never really been known for their performance but lately Samsung been doing a better job at toning down TouchWiz and including beefier specs on their phones and with the galaxy S6. This trend continues with the S6 packing

Samsung's own 64-bit octa-core exynos processor coupled with not two but three gigabytes of ddr4 ram and a u FS 2.0 storage which is basically a geeky way of saying that the Galaxy S6 will be fast and will be one hell of a contender in the phone book style. You may be thinking the galaxy S5 already had a fingerprint scanner why would it be considered a new feature on the Galaxy S6 .Well the S5 fingerprint scanner was a swipe fee scanner where you'd swipe your finger across the home button to unlock your phone and to be perfectly honest it didn't work very well at least compared to the one on the iPhone 5s and iPhone 6 but on the Galaxy s6, Samsung has upgraded the swipe based scanner to a touch based sensor like Apple uses which should translate into a more convenient and hopefully more accurate fingerprint scanner

Samsung pay:

Speaking of the fingerprint scanner the Galaxy s6 will support Samsung pay which will be rolling out later. It'll work similarly to Apple pay on the iPhone with use of the fingerprint scanner and unique transaction tokens to provide more secure payments but the key difference. What's actually exciting about it is it will also support MST or magnetic secure transmission in addition to NFC. What the hell is MST? Basically it's a technology that makes the phone work similarly to the magnetic stripe on your credit card so having this technology built right into the Galaxy s6 means that you'll be able to pay with your phone at about 90% of retailers instead of just these small percentage that currently support NFC. This feature is huge and could be the beginning of the end of the physical wallet.

Camera:

The main camera on the galaxy s6 has these same 16 megapixel resolution that we saw in the s5 but don't let that fool you into thinking that the quality of the camera hasn't changed. The s6 is

Suren lens has been vastly improved now being able to capture more light with an F 1.9 aperture meaning you'll be able to take better quality photos and videos in low-light conditions. The Essex s camera also features optical image stabilization which will help prevent blurry photos due to shaky hands it detected white balance along with an auto HDR mode that intelligently uses HDR for you when the situation calls for it. The auto issuer mode will also be available on the front camera which has been upgraded to a five megapixel shooter with the same f 1.9 aperture. So you'll be able to take your selfies in high resolution even when you're in a low light situation like when you're at a restaurant or a bar.

Charging:

Just like we saw with the note 4 the Galaxy s6 will support super charging allowing you to charge the phone 1.5 times faster than the Galaxy s5 and get up to 4 hours of use after just 10 minutes of charged time on top of that the s5 also supports wireless charging without the need for any special cases. The technology is built right into the phone and will support both of the wireless charging standards so if you see a charging pad at a coffee shop or at a bookstore you won't have to worry about whether or not the phone is compatible. You can just set it down and note that it'll work pretty awesome stuff.

Speaker:

To complement the amazing quad HD display in the galaxy s6, Samsung has worked to improve the audio experience by making these single speaker on the s6 50% louder than the one on the s5. Samsung also moved the speaker from the back of the phone to the bottom which could help prevent it from getting blocked while lying flat on the surface.

Storage:

This new design is definitely a plus but it does come with the cost of having no microSD slot.

So in order to help alleviate this problem, Samsung upgraded the built-in storage to 32 gigabytes for the base model compared to just 16 on the s5. This should help give most people more than enough storage without the need for expansion but if you're somebody who thinks they'll need more storage, Samsung will be offering other models up to 128 gigabytes of storage top new feature.

Software:

Like was mentioned Earlier, Samsung has been lining touch was over the years getting rid of a lot of the gimmicks and useless features and adding features that actually make the user experience better. I think the perfect example of this is what happens when you double press the home button. Before double pressing the home button would launch s-voice not very useful considering you have Google. Now when you double press the home button it launches the camera app in less than a second regardless of what app you're looking at or even if the screen is off, this is actually useful since sometimes you need your camera up and running ASAP to help capture those Kodak moments.

Samsung Galaxy S6: How to Make a Phone Call

If you wanting to add a number, this is how you can do it:

First press on the HOME key to take you back to the home screen and at the bottom dock, there is a phone icon, so tap on the phone and there are different options.

Sometimes you may see windows pop-ups where you can immediately dial on the phone number but sometimes it doesn't show straight away.

There are different ways you can access the phone number e.g. via the log tab. The log tabs contains the recent calls that you have made recently. So you can tap on a number from the log to call, so you can tap on that and then you can tap the phone icon to make the call. You can also tap on other tabs such as a private tab where you have access to all your favorite contacts as well as the contacts tap at the top which will show you all the contacts available on your phone.

So going through the list, you can tap on the contact and then make the call you want or you can simply bring up the dial-pad. To bring up the dial-pad, tap on the small circle at the bottom of your phone, that will bring up the dial pad and from the dial pad you can key in the phone number and start making the call and then tap on the dial button and this will start to make the phone call.

Samsung Galaxy S6: How to Accept or Reject a Phone Call

How to accept a phone call on a Samsung Galaxy s6 edge, so here's an incoming call to our pot. To reject the call, simply tap on hold and slide across to the left and that will reject the phone call. Similarly, to receive and accept the phone call, there is a green icon tap and hold then slide to the right and the call will be picked up and from here you can start talking. you can put on the speaker, you can turn off as well. There's a keypad extra volumes and other things that you could do and to end the call, simply tap on the red button and this will end the call

Samsung Galaxy S6: How to Forward Incoming Call

How to forward incoming call to a different phone number on a Samsung Galaxy s6:

➢ Press the home key at the bottom to go back to the home screen.

➢ Tap on the phone then choose more at the top.

➢ Tap on settings in settings.

➢ Tap on more settings then you will wait to tap on call forwarding so wait for this to finish.

➢ Tap on call forwarding.

➢ Tap on voice call.

The phone will attempt to get the settings from the server. Once you are in there, you will see a field options which you can always forward call to when busy or unreachable

Let's say we want to forward a call when busy, you can choose a contact to forward to or you can simply put in the phone number directly. So let's say I put in a number for instance and then tap enable. So whenever that number is calling my phone, it will immediately forward to a phone number I provided. There's an icon at the top that show like a phone call forwarding icon. This tells you that it is enabled, you can tap on it. You can always turn it off by simply disable it. This you do by just tapping on the icon.

Samsung Galaxy S6: How to Enable / Disable Call Barring for All Outgoing Calls

➢ First tab on the HOME key to go back to the home screen

➢ Tap on the phone couple more times

➢ Choose settings and go down into more settings

➢ Wait for your frontier settings from the network server

➢ Tap on call bearing, tell on voice call

➢ Then at the top, you'll see an outgoing call.

➢ Tap on the switch to turn on.

Once you tap on, you can put in the password as they will require a password to make outgoing call. Simply tap on OK and this should update the settings on the network server. Now depending on your network server, if your network servers do not have the hardware to allow the switches then you will see a fail to wait data call error indicating your network do not allow you to set the call through the handset. Sometimes you can ask them to do it from the network and some network providers will allow you to do it on your handset. So you can use your phone to set the call barrier. This feature will depend on your network ability to give you the option. You can press on the HOME key to go back to the home.

Issue: Can't Make or Receive Calls

Having problems with your call function? Check if the issue lies with your mobile device or the party you're trying to reach. Call someone else and if your call goes through then, the problem isn't with your mobile device. If you still can't get through, check your call forwarding and call barring settings. Search for call settings and under call forwarding just make sure the always forward option is disabled. Under call barring, deactivate all options and check if your SIM card is reading correctly, if not your device will usually alert you with a pop-up or an icon at the top navigation bar on your screen. If you see this, switch off your device remove your SIM card, insert it correctly and switch it back on. Still nothing, see if it works with another mobile device, if it doesn't then, there could be a problem with your SIM card. If the other mobile device can read your SIM card then it's probably likely that your device has a hardware issues. If you're a multi SIM subscriber check if the SIM in use is the primary SIM.

 Go to your settings page and under Wireless or networks make sure your mobile device is not in airplane mode. Once that's done, look for mobile network or more in the settings page enable mobile data and under the network operators tab set it to select networks automatically. Back to the settings page, under mobile network go to network mode and select GSM WCDMA Auto or GSM WCDMA LTE auto.

Press and hold your power button to restart your device. Try updating your software backing up your device and then restoring everything. Go to settings, search for software updates and update your device's operating system to the latest version. To backup and restore, go to Settings select backup and copy your device's files to Google servers. Once your files are backed up just select reset and if this still doesn't resolve the issue then you'll have to get your device checked at your manufacturer's designated care center.

Chapter Two: Text Messaging

How To Access Text Message Settings - Samsung Galaxy S6

To do this just hop into the messages but if it is not on your home screen, click on the app drawer you will find messages there. Go ahead and click on that then clicks on settings you will have your messages settings. From there we can select and change different settings like notifications, we can click on backgrounds and bubbles and we can add nice little themes to our text messages. If we wish, we can also add quick responses. We can use theme like Leicester or we can go ahead and add another just by typing and simply clicking on the plus icon. We can also set up a spam filter by managing spam numbers.

We can manage the spam phrases and look at all your spam messages that the phone has detected. We can also click on more settings which will give us some text messages settings like delivery reports when we have sent a message it will let you know when the recipient has it. We can choose our input by selecting whether we want push messages on or off.

Furthermore, we can use the letter reports for our multimedia messages and read reports that will let us know when a person has received and actually read our message, automatically retrieved messages and set restrictions. In addition, we can also delete old text messages when the maximum number of texts 1000 and multimedia 100 has been exceeded and this will help you save some space but if you wish that to be put off you can simply go ahead and toggle it on or off so that is how you access settings for text messages on the Samsung Galaxy S6.

Samsung Galaxy S6: How to Restore Text Messages

If your phone previously performed my backup then you can restore messages back to your Phone. To restore back your deleted messages, first go back to your home screen by tapping on the home key. Swipe down on the top and tap on the Settings icon on the corner then tap on cloud and accounts. Next tap on Samsung cloud, tap on restore and just wait for a while.

We'll to the move the check box and select all, then go down and tap on messages. We just want to restore messages and other things then tap on restore now. We have to wait for the restore process to complete and then we can check it out to see if all the messages have been restored back to the phone. So basically your phone will back up automatically every 24 hours if you turn on auto backup and using the latest backup. You will recover those messages back to your phone and you can see on your phone attention that the last backup is detected.

How To Send A Picture/MMS Message - Samsung Galaxy S6

To do this all we have to do is access our messaging. If it's not on your home screen, you click on apps and you will find it in the app drawer. So click on messages now and click on the pencil and paper at the bottom right hand corner. It will then ask you to enter your acceptance, go ahead and do this by input the recipient's number. To send your multimedia or picture message click on the paperclip and it will ask you what type of message you would like to send. There are a good few options, if you have any pictures in your library it will give you a few samples of the most recent pictures you have taken and if you would like to access more you click on image then click on photos and it will give you all the pictures that you

have in your gallery.

To add a picture, you simply click on it and it will add the items

below then you simply take your message and all you have to do

now is hit Send and that is how you send a picture or multimedia

message using a Samsung Galaxy s6.

Chapter Three: Tell me how

How to use Physical Home Button As Touch Key Samsung Galaxy S6

It's really simple to set this up. All you need to do is go into your settings to begin with and register your fingerprint.

➢ Go to send

➢ Then to lock screen

➢ Security

➢ Then screen lock type.

Thereafter, go ahead and put your finger print. You'll need to do that in order for it to work. Then go ahead and download the easy home application from the Google Play Store. Open up Google Play and type in easy home. You can download the free version and then open it up and once you've got your fingerprint and everything set up you can hit start.

How To Use Maps/GPS Navigation - Samsung Galaxy S6

How to use maps or GPS navigation on your Samsung Galaxy s6? To do this we are going to have to enable location services by simply slide down from the top. The location table will appear, if we click on it for the first time location services will then be enabled.

Another way of enabling location services is to go into apps .

- ✓ Click on settings

- ✓ Scroll down until you find privacy and safety

- ✓ Click on location and make sure that it as toggled on so to access maps on GPS navigation

- ✓ We go into apps scroll along until we see maps open up

- ✓ Click go to

- ✓ Then all we have to do is to accept Google Maps.

We can search by voice or we can search by a location as well. so if I put and a voice dictation take me to Google swimming pool, it will.

Set Up the SOS Feature on Your Samsung Galaxy S6

Samsung has included a new feature that could be very helpful in an emergency situation in your S6 phone. Basically you select some emergency contacts and if you're ever in a dangerous situation you just press your power button three times then images from your front and back camera will be sent to the emergency contacts. it will also send your exact location as well as an audio recording and a message saying that you need help, so it's effectively a panic button.

For your Smartphone to get started just head to:

➢ The settings menu on your S6.

➢ Choose privacy and safety.

➢ Then tap the send SOS messages entry.

➢ On the next screen go ahead and toggle the switch at the top of the screen to on.

➢ Then take the box near the bottom of the screen and press agrees.

From here it'll inform you that you need to add at least one emergency contact. So press adds on this pop-up then you'll be taken to a list of your contacts. You can choose up to four people from this list and each of them will be contacted when you trigger the SOS. Remember to press done when you have finished selecting your emergency contacts then hit the back button at the top of the screen. From there you can choose what information you would like to send in an emergency situation. Like you can allow it to send pictures audio and even your location and you can as well turn any of these off if you want to.

You should also note that this feature will only work if you're using the default messaging app. If you've set a third-party texting app as your SMS Handler it will not work but when you find yourself in an emergency situation all you have to do now is press your device's power button three times in rapid succession at this point you'll see an ongoing notification that tells you this information is being sent and on the other end they'll get a text message containing pictures from your front and rear camera as well as your location and an audio recording. so it's a nice piece of mind feature that can be of great help if you ever need.

Samsung Galaxy S6 Factory Reset

This process will not affect any Google or Samsung accounts in our phone. To start with

- ➤ Hold power up or a hold volume up button
- ➤ Hold the home button and then hold power button
- ➤ Keep on holding and wait for that screen to come up

➤ Let go so you just wait a bit after it says no command

➤ Then this recovery menu comes up

What you want to do just scroll down with the volume buttons to wipe data/factory reset.

 Now this will erase everything so don't do it if you don't want anything you've erased and hit the Power button. Go down to yes, then it'll do its thing and reboot. It should be reset to factory after the rebooting process is completed.

Chapter Four: Email on Galaxy S6

How to set up your email on your Samsung S6

If you've ever owned an Android device in the past, the process will be similar. If you're a Gmail user you are first prompted to input your email and password when you first set up the phone. So setting up your email has already been done. Now simply tap the Google folder on the home screen and then select Gmail. That's it. You can place the icon for Gmail elsewhere on your phone screen such as at the bottom for easy access. If you use another email provider maybe one from your carrier, your Internet Service Provider, or another webmail client like Yahoo or Outlook.com, you can either use the bundled email app to set up your email, or go straight to the Google Play Store and download a dedicated app for your mail provider.

If you go with the email app already installed on the Galaxy S6 tap it, sign in with your details including your email address and password and the app should find everything else needed to get going.

Alternatively, you can tap manual setup, select the account type like POP3 IMAP or MICROSOFT EXCHANGE ACTIVESYNC and enter in other details when prompted.

Samsung Galaxy S6 How To Add & Delete Email Accounts

To remove email accounts on your Samsung Galaxy S6, just enter in your email then your password and make sure you're connected to the Internet obviously Wi-Fi or whatever. After you do that, you cannot basically choose the sync options for your email and once its set up you can choose whatever you want the name to be. It'll take just a second and will start to load up a bunch of different emails. Let's say you want to add another email account or you want to remove it from your Galaxy S6. What we need to do is go into the settings, scroll down to accounts and then you just click Add Account and you can choose whatever you want it to be. Let's say you want to remove an email account that you don't want, you just click remove account, then a little prompt comes up saying removing the account will delete all of its messages contacts etc just click remove account and then it'll get rid of it and then you won't have that email anymore.

How To Send An Email - Samsung Galaxy S6

You can send an email on the Samsung Galaxy S6 using the Google Account that you set up earlier. To do this all you have to do is go into your Google folder and click on Gmail or you can go into apps then select Gmail from the list. From the Google folder, click on the little pencil in the bottom right hand corner then you can decide whom you would like to send mail to. Enter a subject and write out the email. You can even go ahead and click the paperclip to attach a file or picture. When you are finished all you have to do is click on the little paper airplane and it will send the email to the specified recipient.

Samsung Galaxy S6 Edge: How to Restore Deleted Emails

How to restore accidentally deleted emails on a Samsung galaxy s6.

➢ Press on the HOME key to go back to the home screen.

- ➢ Tap on apps.

- ➢ Tap on emails and from here you want to go to inbox.

- ➢ In your inbox tap on the inbox drop-down list and will pops up all the menu items.

- ➢ Tap on recycle bin (After you deleted your emails it goes to this recycle bin).

From the recycle bin select the mails you want to restore. You may also select any other image that you want to restore back. So make sure you have the checkbox selected, then tap on more and then tap on move now. You want to move back to the inbox and now you can go back to the inbox and your emails have been restored.

Samsung Galaxy S6: How to Enable / Disable Email Sync

How do you enable or disable email sync on a Samsung Galaxy S6?

- ➢ First press on the HOME key to go back to your home screen.

- ➢ Then tap on apps.

- ➢ Tap on email in email when you are in the inbox frame.

- ➢ Tap on more then choose settings in settings.

➤ Tap on the account.

➤ Tap on sync accounts which slightly switch to the left will disable account and slightly switch to the right will enable email sync.

➤ Finally press on the HOME key to finish.

Samsung Galaxy S6: How to Setup New Email Account

Before you can start sending or receiving emails you need to first set up an email account. You can sub emails using services like Gmail, Yahoo Mail, Outlook mail, hotmail, live mail and many others. First go and press on the HOME key to go back to the home screen, and then tap on apps. Go into email in email and under the enter sign in details, input in the email address that you would like to use thereafter, put the password. Tap on next and wait some for the configuration settings from the server and it will apply to this account.

Next we can set the period to sync email for example every two weeks and you can also choose whether to notify you or not when a new email arrives in the inbox. Tap on next, you can give your account a name and I'll tap on done

Samsung Galaxy S6: How to Compose and Send New Email

After you have set up new emails account you can start to send your friend an email.

First press on the home key to go back to the home screen, and then tap on apps go into email and from here you should be in your in inbox. To compose a new email, simply tap on the new email icon and then at the top is the address field so you can type in the address where you want to send email to. Put in the recipient email address, you can put in multiple email address if you want to, then put in the subject of the mail and compose your message. You can also tap on the attach button to attach a photos. You can attach a file, a photo or you can use the camera to take a photo. You can also attach a calendar event, memo; add an audio, contacts details or even a map application. Simply tap on send ugh with all the processes.

Samsung Galaxy S6: How to Embed an Image in Email Signature

How to insert an image into an email signature on a Samsung S6 so that your signature will always be automatically affixed to your composed email. To do this, first we're going to press on the HOME key to go back to the home screen.

> Then tap on apps.

> Tap an email.

> Tap on more. From the pop-up we'll choose settings.

> In settings turn on count them then.

> Turn on the signature option.

> Place the cursor at the location where you want to insert the image.

Now you can either take a picture or you can choose from the gallery and make the necessary adjustment in resizing the image by using adjustment anchor and tap on done when you are through with resizing. Now the messenger has been inserted with an image so if I post a new message you can see the image automatically embedded in it.

Samsung Galaxy S6: How to Block Spam Emails

How to register an email as spam on a Samsung Galaxy S6, first press on the home key to go back to the home screen, then tap on apps, tap an email and in the inbox tap on the email that you want to label as spam, tap on more and choose block the sender. We go to more settings and tap on spam addresses; you can go ahead and add the spam address.

Chapter Five: Contacts

How to add contacts on my Samsung Galaxy S6

The easier way to add a contact is telling the other person to call you. After you have received the call, go to the phone options and locate the number that the other person called you with and select the little face and here we have options where it says create contact or update contact existing in your phone. Select create and input the contact's name and save it. If you want to put more numbers you could do it as well by pressing more, you could as well put an email. There is another option of typing in the contact's number directly but saving the contact through the call log is the easiest way to add a contact.

How to sync Samsung S6 Phone contacts to your Google Account

It's pretty straightforward to backup your contacts to your Google Account on Samsung Galaxy s6. The first thing we need to do is to make sure that we have some contacts on our phone.

The next step is to press on your three little dots at the top to manage contacts and then there's this option here ''move contacts from your phone'' now if you don't have this option just make sure that you've set up your Google account under the settings so if we go back out of here we scroll upwards, click on settings, go down to where you have counter and then accounts again and make sure that you've got your Google account already set-in here. Another thing to mention here is that if you have Auto sync data switched off, you can turn that back on and it will automatically sync everything that's on your phone to your Google account. If it is off by default you actually need to go into the account and press on sync account and then sync your contacts. This is important because otherwise the contacts won't sink if this auto sync data switch is turned off.

Let's go back out to contacts, then we go to our three dots again, manage contacts and then we've got the option of move contacts from phones. So move the contacts saved on your phone to your Google Account, tap on that and then select the Google Account that you want to send it to. To do this, just tap on move and that option will disappear from the menu. So once this is done just go back out again scroll back down and go to your settings, then to your Google account, go into accounts and make sure you go into your Google account that you've backed up. Go to sync account and then tap the sync contacts and you should see it sync there just to make sure that it has actually synced to your Google account.

The next step is to check that the contact has actually uploaded to your Gmail account or your Google account. Go ahead and log into your Google account in your Chrome web browser and then go to the Rubik's Cube little icon there, you click on that and then go down to where it says contacts and click on it and then you should actually get a list of all your contacts that were uploaded.

Samsung Galaxy S6: How to Export Contact List to SIM Card

➢ Press the home key to go back to the home screen.

➢ Tap on contacts.

➢ Tap on the more button at the top and choose settings.

➢ Tap on import/export contacts.

➢ Choose export contacts.

Now choose SIM card and say that information in the name and phone number text will be copy. Some contact information might be lost and the reason this is because your SIM card has very limited memory space. So only important data such as name and phone number is copy any additional other additional details such as email address and photos will not be exported. Now simply tap on the export button and you can choose which types of contacts you want to export then select the contact you want to export and tap on done and then tap on OK and now it is safe to the SIM contacts. Finally press on the HOME key to finish.

Samsung Galaxy S6 : How to Import Contact Detail from SIM Card

> ➢ Press the HOME key to go back to the home screen.

> ➢ Tap on contacts at the bottom.

> ➢ Tap on the more button at the top.

> ➢ Choose settings then tap on import or export contacts.

> ➢ Tap on the import button it will ask you where you want to input it from so choose SIM card.

Now where do you want to save the important contacts – so you can either save it to the device, Google account or Samsung account so choose one of the options, then which contacts you want to import, you can simply select all if you want to import all the contacts and then tap on done.

Samsung Galaxy S6: How to Add a Contact to Favorite Shortcut

With your favorite tabs in place, you can quickly navigate to your contact and easily call them by Just simply go to the favorites and then tap on them. To configure the favorite tab first press on the HOME key to get you back to the home screen then tap on phone. There are two ways of doing this; you'll notice different tabs at the top. Tap on the favorites, then tap on add and here go down the list of contacts and choose the one that you want to add and now if we go back to favorites you'll see that it has been automatically added to the favorites tab.

How to Add or Delete Contacts in Contact groups

To add or delete contacts in contact groups;

- ➢ Open the contacts application.
- ➢ Tap a PPS.
- ➢ Tap contacts.
- ➢ Tap groups.

➢ Select group you want.

➢ Tap Add to add contact.

➢ Check contacts you want to add.

➢ Tap Done.

To delete contacts from group locate the contact you want to delete, tap contacts and tap remove.

Samsung Galaxy S6: How to Remove Duplicate Contacts in Phone Book

There are a number of different ways you can remove duplicate contact on your Samsung S6. First press the home key to go back to the home screen then tap on a contacts app in there, tap more, choose settings and in the settings tap on contact to display. It will shows you all the sources that contacts is pulling info so the contacts app is pulling in the contact details from the device, the SIM card, Google Account, Samsung Account, Facebook and plus any other account that you have added on your phone. So you can choose to listen if you want to simplify your contact list and do not show some duplicate contacts you can just tap on the device to display contacts only on the device and if you check back you can see that the contacts has now been simplified and some of them has been reduced and not duplicated.

Another way to do it is if you have two contacts on the device you can try to merge them together by tapping on more, then tap merge contacts. Another way you can remove the duplicate contacts on your phone is by simply just open up the contacts and have a look at it. If the information is the same or if something is inaccurate you can simply just tap on it and delete it and now you have removed the duplicate contact.

Samsung Galaxy S6 Edge: How to Merge Contacts Into One Record

How you can merge house information from the same contact together into one record, to do this first press the home key to go back to the home screen then tap on the contacts app and then from there tap on a more button at the top and choose merge contacts. The phone will go through your contact list and will find any similar contacts name. So from here you can choose how you want to merge them and then select the contacts that you want to match into one and tap on merge and now they will all become

one contact.

Chapter Six: Browser and Facebook Download

Samsung Galaxy S6 - Browser settings

To set up browser for Samsung Galaxy S6, do the following:

> ➢ From the Home screen tap Internet.

> ➢ Tap more.

> ➢ Tap Settings.

> ➢ To change your home page.

> ➢ Tap homepage.

> ➢ Tap the desired option note e.g. tap other webpage to input the desired home page URL.

> ➢ Enter the desired URL then tap ok.

> ➢ To clear browsing history from the internet settings page tap privacy.

> ➢ Eight tap delete personal data.

> ➢ Select browsing history along with any other desired options then tap delete.

> ➢ To turn pop-up blocking on or off from the internet settings page tap advanced you let him

> ➢ Tap block pop-ups to toggle on/off.

Samsung Galaxy S6: How to Open a New Internet Browser Tab

To open up a new internet browser tap:

> ➤ Press on the HOME key to go back to the home screen.

> ➤ Then tap on internet at the bottom.

> ➤ Tap ''on'' tabs on the bottom, then the top.

> ➤ Tap on new tab, the new tab will be opened up a default
> page and from there you can go to a different page by simply
> typing in the URL.

Samsung Galaxy S6: How to Add a Webpage Bookmark

How to add a bookmark of a web page on a Samsung galaxy S6:

> ➤ First press on the HOME key to go back to the home screen.

> ➤ Then tap on the internet browser at the top in the web
> address of the web page that you want to bookmark once the
> web page has loaded.

> ➤ Check on the more buttons.

> Then tap on add to bookmarks now say the word pressure has been added to bookmarks. if you want to open a bookmark simply tap on the bookmarks.

> Then tap on my device and there you'll see the saves bookmark on your device folder.

> Tap on the bookmark to open the page.

> **Samsung Galaxy S6 Edge: How to Browse Website in Private / Incognito Mode**

> How to open up a new private or internet tab on the internet browser on Samsung Galaxy S6 so if you need to browse in profit so that some of the data is not being recorded on the phone then is how you can open up a new secret tab.

> First press on the home key to go back to the home screen then tap on the internet icon and from there go to tabs, then tap on more and tap on new secret tab. The new secret tab will appear with

> a different color theme. So at the top it's all in grey and when you go to a site you'll see that the progress bar is shown in

yellow so that's how you can open up my new private tab to close it simply tap on tabs and close that private tab.

How To Download & Use Facebook - Samsung Galaxy S6

How to download and add your Facebook account to the Samsung Galaxy s6 . To do this we simply go into the Play Store application itself. That may not be on your home screen. To get to the play store, simply go into apps then you will see the Play Store in there. Click on it then click on the search bar at the top and type in Facebook and that will appear in the top searches, click on it and allow it to install. When it's downloaded simply click open and the app will open up and from here you can go ahead and enter your username and password and log in.

Chapter Seven: Entertainment Application

Samsung Galaxy S6: How to Take a Virtual shot With Camera

How do you take a virtual shot with your camera on a Samsung Galaxy S6? With virtual shot you can take a photo and will take your camera around the room and will allow you to take the pictures at different angle.

First, press on the HOME key to go back to the home screen and then tap on apps and choose Camera. Once the camera has launched a pond mod at the bottom, choose virtual shot but if what you want is not available in the list you need to go and tap on the download button and this will allow you a dialogue. Click more and this will load more different mode onto your phone. So choose virtual shot and here now first point to where you want to start and tap on the camera icon and then continue to take the phone slowly so that the camera could capture all the pictures hopefully once you're satisfy with your position, just tap on the stop button. You can continue to keep going if you want to or you can just press on stop where you want to stop the pictures. Now   tap on the preview icon and then tap on the virtual icon. With virtual you can basically take the phone to the left or to the right to view the picture.

Samsung Galaxy S6: How to Enable / Disable Camera Video Stabilization

If you like to think of other videos and you want to have stabilized videos then you can turn this feature on. First press on the home key to go back to the home screen, then tap on apps and then go to camera and tap on the Settings icon at the top, then from the choose video stabilization from the part menu. Tap on the switch to turn on/off sliding, the switch to the left will disable this big feature and sliding the switch to the right would turn it on. Finally, press on the HOME key to go back to your home screen or you can tap on the back key at the top to go back to the camera.

How To Record A Video - Samsung Galaxy S6

To do this we have to start the camera up by going into the apps and click on camera. From there we click on the little video icon next to the main shutter button and you are recording a video already. Simply click stop when you are finished and the video will then be saved to your gallery. So go to your gallery to check on the saved video.

Galaxy S6 / S6 Edge: How to Delete Photos, Videos, & Albums

Firstly thing is go to your gallery app, you may have several albums here, now if you want to delete the whole album what you can do is long press any one of these albums, check the album and go ahead and delete. You can select multiple albums and delete them all at once as well. Let's say you go into one of your albums in the gallery and there's one picture you want to delete what you simply do is just click on that picture and tap on delete button. To delete multiple photos and videos what we simply do is to long press any one of your photos or videos and start selecting each one of them individually then click on delete button and they are gone.

Chapter Eight: playing music and video

How To Use Music Player - Samsung Galaxy S6

To do this all we have to do is go into the apps then simply select the music player. All your music that is on database (if you have any) will be listed. You can go into playlists and it will give you any playlists that you have. Create a new playlists by clicking on create and give it a name. You now have a playlist, all your music would pop up and you can simply check the box to add it to your new playlist and when you have finished, simply click done. If you go back, you can go into tracks and it will give you a list of all your tracks.

a few relate to quick search as you'll notice an alphabet down the seed you would just simply click on the letter and it would skip to any artists that begin with this letter or tracks that begin with that letter. You can also go into genres folders composers and search that way or you can click the search button up the top and simply take the name of the artist or song that you are looking for.

Samsung Galaxy S6: How to Shuffle Your Music to Play Randomly

To do this press on the HOME key to go back to the home screen, and then tap on apps, tap on music. From here, open up the playlist and play one of the songs. So choose one of the songs, you can open this up at the bottom left corner. You can tap on the shuffle icon to toggle the state between on and off. If you want to slower after a shuffle, tap on that and the music will play randomly. Press on the HOME key to go back to your home screen.

How To Connect Headphones/Aux Cable - Samsung Galaxy S6

To insert or connect an auxiliary cable or headphones into the Galaxy s6, take the headphone jack and on the bottom left hand corner of your device you will find the headphone port simply take the jack and push it all the way in. As simple as that, that is how to connect headphones or audio cables to the Samsung Galaxy s6.

How To Pair and Connect Bluetooth Headset With Samsung Galaxy S6

You can actually pair a Bluetooth headset with the Samsung Galaxy S6 i.e. any Samsung Bluetooth headset, a Sony Bluetooth headset or jab on Bluetooth headset. To put the Samsung Bluetooth headset look for day on/off an answer key while the Bluetooth headset is off, press on button and keep pressing the button, it will go into pairing mode right there that's the first thing. In the case of the Sony Bluetooth headset is the same thing. It has more keys on it volume mute, you look for the answer key which is the same as the on/off key press on it again it will turn on first and then after a couple of seconds you will go into pairing mode.

In the case of the jawbone Bluetooth headset is a little different it only has two keys, the answer key on the back and the on/off switch so you press the answer key. keep pressing on it and then you turn on the Bluetooth headset and it will go into pairing mode again right now the device we have the Bluetooth headset into pairing mode, whichever you have now we unlock the screen then we go to apps or applications based on settings. Press on connections, now press on Bluetooth then we turn on Bluetooth right there. Now click on the check mark to make the phone itself visible to all Bluetooth devices and press the scan. You scan for any Bluetooth devices nearby especially those that are into pairing mode. Click on the jawbone icon and pair once the Bluetooth connection have been detected.

Now go to the home screen and press the answer key for a while

and then release the key. You will go into voice commands and you

can start to use it.

Chapter Nine: Voice Assistant

Samsung Galaxy S6 Edge: How to Take a Photo With Voice Command

How do you take a photo with voice control on a Samsung Galaxy S6 camera? First press the HOME key to go back to the home screen then tap on apps and then tap on camera. In the camera, tap on the Settings icon at the top and this will display the camera settings menu. Go down and tap on the voice control turn it on. Once it is on, you can take a picture by saying smile, cheese, capture. The key word here is ''capture''.

Samsung Galaxy S6: Text Messaging Using Your Voice

Whenever you want to use your voice to text message on Samsung Galaxy s6, you just open up a text message conversation and click the little microphone button and start talking. Whenever you want to end the message that you're using your voice with, you just got to click the X button.

Chapter Ten: Using Calendar

How To Sync Calendar - Samsung Galaxy S6

Sync calendar with an online account such as Google account on Samsung Galaxy S6 is a simple task. What we have to do is go into S Planner as that is what calendar is called on the Galaxy devices. Simply click on it, click more in the top right hand corner then click on manage. If you wish to add another account simply click Add Account and it will allow you to add account and this will sync your calendars to all your online accounts.

Samsung Galaxy S6: How to Create a New Calendar Event

First press the HOME key to take you back to the home screen then tap on apps and turn on S planner. The S planner is the actual calendar on your phone; you can create a new meeting event. It shows you the current month and you can tap on the day that you want to create the event. For example if you want to create the event on Monday just tap on that day once and start. If you tap on it twice it will create the event automatically for you. You can create a new event by tapping on the plus icon.

So there are a few different ways you can do it. To make it easy just double tap on that day and then it shows the day, you can give the event a title. You can just say meeting and then you choose a start date and end date. So if you tap on it and choose when the event will start for example you want to start the meeting at 12 o'clock then you'll tap on done then you choose when it ends, by default it is a one-hour event. Let's say if this meeting goes on for two hours you can set it for 14:00 and then tap on done. So now that we have set the start and end date you can also choose which calendar to type this one to, then you can also set a reminder by default it's a one hour notifications.

If you want to add more notification reminder, you can tap on the plus icon and choose when the notification will start. For example, you can choose one day before and you can see added to notifications one day before and one hour before. You can also choose the location if you wanted to or you can leave it blank. You can tap on map to locate the locations. You can even put in the street name and the house number if you wanted to be more specific. At the bottom are different options, so this add the option for repeated events you can invite other people to the meetings as well. You can also add a note and set a time zone. Once you're happy with all the settings and details you go ahead and tap on save at the top and you'll save the event to the calendar.

How To Edit & Delete A Calendar Appointment - Samsung Galaxy S6

Calendar on the Galaxy devices is known as S Planner. So to access this we simply go into apps from there you will select S planner. Let say you already have an appointment made, So to edit, click on it and will allow you to go in and edit. You can edit whatever you like. Click Save after you've finished editing and the name will have changed. If you want to delete it you simply click X and it will be deleted.